It's
All
About.
You

A Young Adult's Guide for Positive Living

Thomas L. Barksdale, II

The Barksdale Foundation

The Barksdale Foundation

Library of Congress Card Cataloging Data: 97-69498

Barksdale, Thomas, L., 1974-
  It's All About You
  1. Youth 2. Motivation for youth 3. Inspiration
  4. African-American youth 5. Self-help/Self-development for youth

ISBN: 1-887798-09-9

For additional information or should you have any comments or suggestions, please write or call:

> The Barksdale Foundation PO BOX 26980
> Charlotte, NC 28221-704-598-8691
> or log on to www.barksdalefoundation.com

This work is dedicated to my parents, Thomas and Hurlyn, who provided and taught me about life and who loved me unconditionally. Also, without the support of my three sisters, Angie, Shandi, and my twin Taiwan, I would not have been able to forge ahead. I love each of you dearly.

And to all of the youth of America, this work is also dedicated.

Thank You!

S everal people helped me in the writing process. However, there are two people who spent many hours editing and giving me final suggestions. They are Dr. Wil Brower, founder of Wil Brower and Associates, and Dr. Jane Brown, Associate Professor of English at North Carolina A&T State University.

These two individuals spent many days sharing ideas and expertise that provided invaluable knowledge. Without them this work would have never been produced. I thank the two of you for your feedback and support which helped me to complete this project. The two of you gave me the confidence to continue and persevere. You will never be forgotten.

Teachers, professors and students of Lincoln Middle, Dudley High and North Carolina A&T State University, thank you for teaching me the basics. To all members of Alpha Phi Alpha Fraternity, Inc., especially members of Beta Epsilon, your sup-

Thank You!

port carried me. To Dudley Products, Inc., thank you for training me early in my understanding. Also, the Episcopal Church of The Redeemer, built my spiritual foundation which I appreciate.

To the following families, thank you for your individual coaching throughout my life: The Banks, Bailey's, Castelow's, Artist Brothers, Crews, Davis's, Fikes, Gwynns, Hughes, Ingram's, Johnson's, Lambert's, Peele's, Richardson's, Shears, Starks, Stewarts, Stubbs, Vaughn's, Wade's, Walkers and Williams.

Several individuals must be mentioned: Nigel Alston, Bailey Brothers, Jay Banks, Greg Bush, Ray Cooke, Steve Devoe, Teri Emehel, Dale Fisher, Felicia Gatson, Joyce Johnson, Tracey Jarman, Wil Jones, Akbar Majeed, Bernard Morgan, Rich McCloskey, Rev. Carlton Morales, Jamal Shears, Michael Simmons, Al Twitty, Harold Willis, Deborah Underwood and the Williams Brothers. Thank you!

Finally, I express my sincere appreciation for the time and attention given to my work by the staff at Duncan & Duncan, Inc. You were unwavering in your quest to present a unique and quality product. A special thanks also goes to Richard Jones for his artistic work on the illustrations.

All of you have made my tomorrow brighter. I am glad to have met you in this special life. Again, thank you so much and I wish you God's speed.

Thomas L. Barksdale, II

Foreword

*I*t's *All About You* is an encouraging look at self. Youths often give up on themselves because others have forgotten them. Thomas Barksdale has not forgotten. He remembers when he was a child and the people that played key roles in his life and who gave him positive reinforcement. Barksdale vividly illustrates experiences that shaped his life that could help today's young adults avoid some of the same pitfalls.

At a time when the media stereotypes youth, especially African-American males, as gangsters, Barksdale uses his book to encourage them to shatter the media's portrayal.

Across the nation, young lives are dramatically altered by bad decisions and poor choices. *It's All About You* teaches youth in a conversational tone that the choices they make while growing up have a long-lasting effect.

Foreword

The topics covered provide realistic examples and solutions to many of the problems that young people face today. At its core, this book is about preparation and follow-through. It's easy for any young person to stray off the course and get lost without any objectives in life. With poignant stories, Barksdale shows readers how to grow through difficulties, fears and struggles.

A series of self-examinations throughout the book allows readers to survey themselves in an attempt to better understand their unique qualities and God-given gifts.

This book is the counseling big brother young adults need. Barksdale draws from critical situations in his own life and others to prove that personal mastery and self-esteem are vital components in actualizing what young adults want to achieve in life.

To make it better for the next generation, it's essential that all of us at some point commit to investing time in our youth. Barksdale understands his role in the restoration of a "lost generation." He's not afraid to tackle thought-provoking issues that concern every young adult on a level the reader will be able to comprehend and follow without difficulty.

It's All About You is not a selfish statement. It's an announcement to the world that you are going to do everything within your reach to make your life and the lives of those around you run a little smoother.

Betsy Peoples
Emerge Magazine

Between the Pages

Introduction

U pon graduating from North Carolina Agricultural and Technical State University, I knew working in corporate America was not my top priority. After interning and co-oping for a major firm, I learned very quickly my talents stretched far beyond an office. So I decided to follow my dream: to become a Motivational Speaker professionally. I have been in this business for about five years and I'm honored to have had the opportunity to reach many young adults through speeches and seminars.

After diversifying my business into Educational Consulting, I decided my message had the potential to reach far more young adults if I wrote an effective and thought-provoking book. So I sat and started writing, *It's All About You.*

What follows is a series of chapters explaining the critical issues that are faced by young adults. Personal stories which maintain a sense of humor to grasp the reader's attention are displayed. It is my hope that you will learn that personal mastery and self-esteem are critical concepts for a successful life. Each reader, at points along the way, will be called to answer several questions honestly. The reader will begin to understand the emotional and social components of human development. Several books are cited to entice young people to seek further understanding of these lessons. Although this book is a Self-Help/Motivational piece for young people, adults can vastly benefit.

My being a twenty-three year old black man will serve as an example to the youth of America. It shows that with hard work and effective effort, you too can make it. If you decide today to set realistic, measurable and attainable goals, life can and will be a big play ground. If young people master these concepts, the future will be as bright as a new sun.

It's All About You stresses that without a clear understanding of self, your potential can be lost forever. This work will explore the human soul and cause you to learn from every fiber of your being. It also encourages young adults to take an active part in their lives by seeking to understand, then to be understood. Learning all you can as often as you can will foster opportunities that otherwise would be foreign.

This book talks directly to young adults. Its purpose is to

give a broader understanding of issues young people face daily. My intentions are for young adults to use this book as a starter tool to aid in their development. By focusing on real-life stories, you will be able to pinpoint some of your own experiences and provide your mind with food for thought.

When you can tell your mind that you love being who you are, success is attainable. Responsibility, confidence, love, success, empowerment and respect are stressed as you travel throughout this book. When you begin to understand that *it's all about you,* despite your background or present situation, opportunities will begin to come your way. After reading this work, I sincerely hope that you will never accept being an average person. Here we go!

Thomas L. Barksdale, II

One

Acceptance

If you can't find peace and happiness within yourself, you're not likely to find it in others.

—Wil Brower, Ph.D.

I t was in the fifth grade that I discovered I had a strong need for acceptance. My mother, a very beautiful woman, bought me a pair of light blue, high-top, strapped, tennis shoes. I received her gift with great joy, but soon found myself frustrated because I had not received the "OK" from my friends to wear them. One particular morning, I woke up determined that this was the day I would show my peers what my mother had bought. I packed my shoes ever so tightly in my bookbag and set off for school.

As the day passed, I grew worried about how my shoes would be received. Thinking back, I experienced anxiety, tension and other emotions that described my need for acceptance. Finally, I told one of my friends I had something to show him. He was very interested and agreed to take a look. When I opened my bookbag, I felt as if the whole world was watching, although it was just the two of us. As I pulled the shoes from my bag, silence erupted like still water. My homeboy said, "Man, those shoes are bad (meaning good). Where did you get them?"

I immediately smiled and thanked God that my mother had made an excellent choice. Thereafter, I replaced my Wild Styles (Imitation Adidas) with my new shoes.

What are some of the lessons we can learn through this simple but profound story? Firstly, let's remember that all of us, young and old, have a strong need for acceptance, honor and praise. As children, our innermost beings were bundles of ego. When tested in a negative fashion, we guarded ourselves against those forces and used behavior that acted as defense mechanisms. We like being liked and we love being loved. So often this burning desire causes us to succumb to amnesia as it relates to our own thoughts and belief systems.

Secondly, as adults we have a vested interest in being popular, important and respected by people in our circle of influence. Human tendencies cause us to focus on being accepted by our peer group. Sometimes peer pressure influences us to decrease the worth we place on our own values and judgements.

Couldn't I have just placed on my feet what my mother provided for me? Who was I to seek approval from a friend when my mother and father had already given me the love and support I needed? If my friend had said that he didn't like my shoes, I probably would have gone home angry with my mother for buying me something my friend didn't like. So often we go through life inviting others to give us advice, acknowledgment and support without listening to ourselves. I often tell young people that the first foreign language we take is our own, spoken by our lips.

One day, my best friend and I developed a plan to destroy a building other neighborhood buddies had constructed. He was eleven years old and I was twelve. We decided that since they would not let us play with them in their new club house, we would destroy it. The first phase of the plan was to agree and commit to each other. We shook hands and proceeded to phase two. Next, a decision had to be made as to the day and time we would engage in this self-defeating behavior. The third phase was rather simple: we adopted the old Nike adage, "Just Do It."

So, here we were participating in negative behavior only because we felt left out of the "mainstream," almost like the oppressed (BLACK) people in America. I remember feeling excluded, cheated and shunned from my neighborhood clique. My friends told us that in our presence they felt out of place, like flowers that grow with weeds. It hurt us so badly; we became determined to get back.

As we approached the beautiful construction, my heart was beating like a drum cadence with continuous rhythm. With rocks and other objects in our hands, we threw them like a quarterback throws a football to a wide receiver with professional precision. Minutes passed, and soon our arms rested high above our heads; we were victorious. Why did we think we had won? Now I understand that Kyle and I were prisoners in our own minds. Self-inflicted cataracts blinded us from practicing the home training that our parents had worked so diligently to teach us.

In life, at some point all of us engage in behaviors that are not representative of who we really are. We do it because we want to be recognized and accepted. How we deal and cope with these feelings will have an ultimate impact on our level of success and prosperity.

As young people, we already possess the tools with which

we can build. Just look in the mirror. There was a story told by Russell Conwell, founder of Temple University and a famous lecturer, of a farmer named Ali Hoffitt. Hoffitt discovered he had a burning desire to acquire diamonds. He sold all of his land and traveled the world searching for his obsession. He spent all of his money and energy in his quest. Ali soon found himself in a state of deep depression and threw himself in the ocean. He committed suicide. Our only guess is he committed suicide because he never found diamonds.

But folks, it was on the very farm that Hoffitt had lived that the biggest diamond mine in the world was discovered. All he had to do was look in his own back yard and he would have found acres of diamonds. And so it is with you. Look at yourself for acceptance, honor and praise. Public opinion matters when running for office, but not when finding self. Your richness and greatness lies within you. The poem, *The Man in the Glass*, illustrates this point.

The Man in the Glass

When you get what you want
in the struggle for self
and the world makes you King for a day,
go to the mirror and look at yourself
and see what that reflection has to say.

It's All About You

For it isn't your mother, father,
girlfriend, and boyfriend
whose judgment upon you must pass,
the person's verdict who counts most
in your life is the one staring back in the glass.

Some people may think you are a straight
shootin' chum and call you a wonderful guy,
but the man in the glass says you're only a bum
if you can't look him straight in the eye.

He is the person to please
never mind all of the rest
for he's clear with you to the end,
and you know you have passed your
most dangerous difficult test if
the man in the glass is your friend.

For you may walk down the
whole pathways of life
and get pats on your back as you pass,
but your final reward will be filled
with heartaches and tears
if you cheated the man in the glass.

—Author Unknown

Oftentimes, a man or woman travels all over in search of what is needed and returns home to find it. I challenge each of you today to look to yourself for your acceptance and value. I dare you to be great. *It's all about you.*

Two

Negative Thinking

Some people are so negative that to never see them again in life is too soon. —Les Brown

As young people, we often find ourselves without goals or aspirations. This happens not because we are intellectually deficient or inferior; it happens because we do not believe in ourselves. Our minds lie in the ruin of existence which induces us to do nothing and rest afterwards. We often play negative tapes in our minds that feed us no confidence, hope or perseverance. Often this causes us to disengage in learning, therefore, we cheat ourselves of opportunities to achieve.

It's incumbent upon us that we control what enters and exits our minds. "One of the richest places on earth," Marion Barnes, my personal mentor, once said, "is the graveyard." So many people die with their dreams unfulfilled and their goals unaccomplished. This happens not because they lack ability, but because they tell themselves they can't. Alas, we often find ourselves allowing others to influence us to become helpless, powerless and hopeless. Our parents, teachers and friends often treat us like we're incapable. And so we start acting out what we learned from these "authorities."

There was an elementary school teacher who told her class they could not read and she didn't expect them ever to read. After the story was released to the press, one youngster told reporters, "My teacher told me I could not read, so why should I try?" It is in situations like these where we find ourselves most vulnerable. Negative thinking and low expectations are the root cause of failure-oriented people.

How do we practice positive thinking? Despite what others tell us, how can we believe in our God-given ability? Self-awareness and fortitude will enable us to penetrate the forces that attack our souls like cancerous cells. One day I told a group of my associates that I was going to become a motivational speaker. They laughed and told me I couldn't do it. But I believed in myself and now I'm doing it. A positive attitude will teach us that we can become anything we choose if we apply ourselves.

Sir Edmund Hillary was the first man to successfully climb Mount Everest, the largest mountain in the world. He failed on several early attempts and even left five of his associates dead on one side of the mountain. The Parliament of his native country honored him with a banquet for his enormous effort. They even bought a large picture of Mount Everest and placed it on the wall. Sir Edmund entered the facility and watched as his fans rose for a standing ovation. Consumed in the moment, Hillary wept in a fitful state. The Parliament and guests thought his acts were of joy; but they soon found themselves incorrect. Sir Edmund literally ran to the picture hanging on the wall and started pounding the frame and said, "You defeated me, Mr. Mountain, but you won't defeat me anymore, because you have stopped growing, but I am still growing."

This story illustrates an individual with determination. The positive thinking of his situation allowed him to accept his current position but to implement strategies to overcome it. That is how we overcome negative thinking. Relaxing, and carefully evaluating our situations are ways in which we grow and develop. The late Reverend Dr. Norman Vincent Peele said i best, "When you see a problem coming down the road, holler, 'Hello problem, where have you been? I've been training for you all of my life.'" It is this idea, and others, that feed us the nutrients of unlimited power over life's daily obstacles and tribulations. We all possess keys for unlocking our positive potential.

Decide today that you will feed your mind with positive thought, that you will forgive yourself for starring in a play called self-limiting expression, and start progressing toward greatness. Pamper your consciousness, and reward yourself for your successes, and learn from your failures. It is your responsibility to strive toward personal mastery, leaving behind negative thinking. *It's all about you.*

Three

Difficulties

Life is difficult, this is a great truth,
one of the greatest truths.
It is a great truth because once we truly see this
truth, we transcend it. Once we truly
know that life is difficult, once we
truly understand and accept it,
then life is no longer difficult.
Because once it is accepted,

the fact that life is difficult
no longer matters.
—*Scott Peck*

H ave you ever been in a situation where you were having extreme difficulty and perhaps you thought the world was against you? Maybe you asked God why He wasn't present when you were being created. In these times it seemed that life dealt you a bad hand. If these attitudes sound familiar, it is because all of us will, at some point in time, question the fairness of life. We always seem to ask "why?" We wish bad circumstances not on others, just not on us.

We often tell ourselves that things will get better and faith will allow us to endure. For young people, these feelings are ever so common. School, parents and friends are our greatest challenges. These subjects often are not addressed because young people cannot find venues to articulate their feelings. As adults, we tend to worry and we become so terribly stressed out.

Think about all the people you interact with everyday, week, month and year—all the people we pass while driving. These individuals are carrying difficulties that weigh heavy on the heart, mind and spirit. Some deal and cope with these situations through avoidance, others through negative behaviors or internalization. We tell ourselves we deserve better and we hope for a brighter day. But how can we expect different results when we act, feel and think in the same realm of understanding?

One of the best ways to solve difficulties is to change. Some people are too afraid to get out of the box. Tunnel vision is their middle name. Life is more meaningful than that. Stop and think. Sometimes our failures are predictable. When a challenging situation confronts us, feeble-minded individuals drop out of life. They surrender themselves to morbid forces. You know people who are so low on themselves that a snake has to look down to see them. They have allowed their difficulties and problems to live within them.

Today, decide that you will deal with your difficulties head on and recognize that life's clock is ticking away. Dr. James Dobson once said, "Live until you die." A friend of mine told me about his grandmother's comments on her long life. He said, "Tommy, the other day grandma told me she was tired; she had done everything she wanted to do." Folks, I encourage you to use life up. Every time you wake up you have another shot in life. Difficulties will always surface. Accept this as one of life's programs. Stand up! Sitting down over time produces sores worth nothing. DEAL WITH IT. *It's all about you.*

Four

Understanding

How far you go in life depends on your being tender with the young, compassionate with the aged, sympathetic with the striving, and tolerant with the weak and the strong. Because someday in life you would have been all of these. —George W. Carver

D o we understand our parents? Do we understand our peers? What about our teachers and civic leaders? Do they understand us? These are all very important questions that sometimes remain unanswered like a telephone ringing when no one's home. Can people live in the same house for many years and never know each other? What about the clubs and organizations that we belong to? Is it possible to be involved in activities that you know nothing about?

Think about the ways in which you assess your situations. Often, we make decisions without a clear understanding of the matters at hand. We add, delete, or exaggerate the facts. All of these human tendencies are the result of understanding the issues. Carefully and rationally thinking through experiences saves us from further hurt, pain or strife.

Patience is one key to understanding. Generally we all want things instantly. When I was in fourth grade my class took a spelling test. I was the first one to finish and was confident I got an A. When the teacher returned the test, I found I had scored lower than the neighborhood speed limit. It wasn't that I didn't know how to spell, I simply rushed through the exam. How many of you have rushed through an experience? Forgetting to take your time and rushing is guaranteed failure.

Another key to proper understanding is reading effectively. Jonathon Kozol told of a story in his book, *Illiterate America,* in which a mother bought a gallon of Crisco Oil for her family for dinner. The woman saw a picture of fried chicken on the label and thought she was buying chicken. Your ability to read and effectively communicate increases your understanding. Are you tolerant of people? Do you take time to understand why people behave and think a certain way? One poem that I like explains why an individual chose to indulge in what he believed.

It Matters To This One

As I walked along the seashore
This young boy greeted me.
He was tossing stranded starfish
Back to the deep blue sea.
I said, "Tell me why you bother,
Why waste your time this way,
There's a million stranded starfish
Does it matter, anyway?"
And he said, "It matters to this one,
It deserves a chance to grow.
It matters to this one,
I can't save them all you know.
But it matters to this one.
I'll return it to sea.
It matters to this one,
And it matters to me."

I walked into a classroom,

The teacher greeted me.
She was helping Johnny study,
He was struggling I could see.
I said, "Tell me why you bother,
Why you waste your time this way.
Johnny's only one of millions,
Does it matter, anyway?"
And she said, "It matters to this one,
He deserves a chance to grow.
It matters to this one,
I can't save them all, I know.
But, it matters to this one,
I'll help him to be what he can be.
It matters to this one,
And it matters to me."

—Author Unknown

Clearly, we are beginning to understand why people engage in activities that matter to them. We often listen to one radio station in life WIIFM (What's In It For Me?). This orientation is dangerous because we soon find ourselves wrapped up in self; ignoring the very people who have supported and sacrificed for us. We all need each other. Think about Siamese twins: without each other they die.

Diversity issues are realities that impede or prevent us from

Understanding

respecting differences and understanding. Historically, factions have assigned people to dominant and subordinate groups or classes. There is no one group that is genetically inferior to another. This absurd verbal and written persuasion only continues because of lack of understanding.

I contend, until we make a sincere effort to understand human wants and needs, we will always question and ponder if we are doing the things that we should be doing. Seek proper understanding. *It's all about you.*

Five

Accepting Defeat

Press on. Nothing can take the place of persistence. Talent will not; the world is full of unsuccessful people with talent. Genius will not; unrewarded genius is almost a proverb. Education alone will not; the world is full of educated derelicts. Persistence and determination alone are omnipotent. —Calvin Coolidge

When is the last time you failed at something? Were

you completely down on yourself? Did those negative tapes play in your mind? Were you so bent out of shape you faked being successful? Is there a difference between a winner or loser?

What makes a winner win? Winners, like everyone else, fear failing. They question their ability, intelligence and effort. They hurt, hear no constantly and even waste time worrying. These people, when getting started, often don't recognize their qualities. Some people feel there is only one particular group ordained by God to win. Some people think only pretty people win, that only smart people win, that only those born with "silver spoons in their mouths" win. People with fancy degrees and titles are often predicted to win. Individuals who are labeled elite are destined to win. Geographical location determines if a person wins. All of these reasons have no more value than a condemned house.

People are successful when they don't accept defeat. These people recognize early that they must paint their own picture. They believe that the word success should have as many meanings as people in the world. Winners don't wish to be like others. They don't wish to be prettier than other people. They don't compare their cognitive ability with others. Most winners believe their house is big enough; that their wife's wedding ring is expensive enough; that their school clothes are just fine. They don't succumb to peer pressure. If you don't like them, they may still like you. Winners believe that when a teacher, business client, parent or any other person tells them no, it's only because they did not give them enough information to make a sound decision. These folks know and believe they have the ability. Winners just want their shot. When they die they want people to say, "There lived someone who went up against life and won."

People often talk about winners. Among young people, those who win often live life like a 100 meter sprinter. They must perform and suffer by themselves. In these years, they are exposed to verbal abuse. For example, my twin sister, Taiwan, won a spelling bee. Our parents were very proud, but Taiwan couldn't fully enjoy her accomplishment. Her friends and foes called her nerd, smarty, brainy and teacher's pet. Although she won, she still felt defeated. It is your ability to believe in what you do that makes you successful.

My fraternity sponsored an oratorical contest in which I represented the undergraduate chapters from North Carolina. Right before it was my time to speak, I told myself, "Man, look at all these people you have the opportunity to teach." As I walked up to the lectern and looked over my audience, I remember telling myself, "I'm gonna let it all hang out." I spoke from the heart and when I finished the crowd roared. I sat down satisfied with my presentation.

People came to congratulate me and told me they knew I'd won. Although the winner wouldn't be announced until the

next morning, I knew I was the best that day. The next morning the organizer started issuing the awards. He started with the
first runner up of the oratorical contest, and guess what; he
announced my name. He said, "First runner-up, Thomas L.
Barksdale, II." Everybody had thought I would be the top winner, not the first runner up! The gentleman who won told me
before the award's banquet started, "Brother, you did a wonderful job. I know you are going to represent us well at the na-
tional convention."

When my name was called, I looked at one of my chapter
brothers, Ed Zimmerman, and said, "You've got to be kidding
me."

And to add insult to injury, they expected me to walk up
and receive a plaque that I had not earned. Imagine how I felt
with all those people clapping not because of how I spoke, but
because they felt sorrow for me. That was one of the longest
walks in my life. It still had not dawned on me that I had lost.
I was mad and upset until I realized those were feelings of defeat.

Even when you perform well in all that you do, sometimes
you will not win in the conventional sense. For various reasons
you may come in second, third or fourth. But how you feel
about what you do determines whether you are successful. I
didn't really need to be told by others I spoke well that day; I
knew it. If I had told myself I was a failure, I might have never

tried to speak again. All of us, at some time in our lives, will experience similar situations. We must maintain our ability to believe that in all things we are winners.

What is a loser? A loser is someone who has ability but accepts defeat. The only real difference between a winner and loser is how they deal with experiences. Losers believe that life owes them a break. They often make the association that they're never lucky. They spend time playing the lottery rather than working. When actors on soap operas have a bad day, they have a bad day. When a particular rapper gets sick, these types of people get sick.

Losers often talk the same stuff. "Man, did you hear what SHAQ signed for?"

Losers walk in their friend's house and say to themselves, "My TV is 10 inches wider than this."

Among young people, losers are those who pretend to be stupid or dumb. They compare what they mentally possess with material possessions of others. People who like to lose often get angry about progress. Loser-oriented people hate to be by themselves.

Losers encourage people to become helpless and question their ability. These people live a life full of myths. Here is the question: Which one are you? Are you a winner or are you a loser? If you had to define yourself by an alphabet, would you place yourself before A or after Z? I'm waiting for your answer.

Accepting Defeat

Whatever you decide, it is your responsibility to live a life of pride and respect. I assert that everyone wants to be somebody. No one starts out not wanting to be anything. So what we know is that failure, defeat and hate are learned. People make choices to live this way. Take time to evaluate your talents and maximize your greatness.

This is extremely difficult for those of us who have systematically been oppressed. Blacks, as well as other groups, have labored long hours in search of equality. For some young Blacks, just to make it to school is a success. Political, economic and social constraints often hamper Blacks from certain opportunities. Winning, thus becomes a whole new meaning for Blacks. Some people who belong to this group believe if they provide for their families they win. Young members feel that just staying out of jail makes them win. If they attend school, whether they learn or not, they win. Fighting often means that they win. All of these factors, and many more become measures which affect how they live.

Some Black youths get so much advice, they often engage in activities in which they never care to participate. Think of all of those young people who go to college to please their parents. It's hard for them to be successful because they don't want to be there. We have to expose black children at an early age to the importance of cognitive development. Alas, the emotional and social component must be addressed.

Decide for yourself what your measures for winning are, and then write them down. But never, ever accept defeat. If your outcomes don't turn out as you want them to, do everything a little bit more. Study more. Read books more. Respect family, friends and teachers more. Think and inwardly digest more. Just run a little bit faster. *It's all about you.*

Six

Friendship

The friend of a fool is a fool. The friend of a wise person is another wise person. —Husia

F riendships are so crucial in life. It is often said that a friend is someone who knows everything about you and still wants to hang around you. How many true friends do you have? I bet you can count them on one hand. Why is this so? Many times it is because people are jealous and start gossiping. They wish they could be just like you and when they find that it's not possible, they have no other recourse (option) but to talk behind your back. Bennie Brewington, one of my fraternity brothers, told me, "People have to be close to you to stab you in the back." That is so true.

Relationships between people falter because of competition. We compete with how we dress, who we date and even others with whom we choose to hang around. One disagreement causes our friendships to suffer. These minute differences destroy some of the closest bonds ever made. People who were thought to be very close never speak again in life. Then others talk up what has happened and perpetuate further disenchantment.

How can we guard against these and other destructive happenings? Firstly, let's stop the gossiping. People know when you are talking about them. Your behavior changes. You look at them in a different way. As a result, the support and respect you once displayed isn't there.

Secondly, learn to value people with whom you spend the most time. Generally, your first friends are those who grow up in your neighborhood. Love these people because, after all, they know a lot about you. Some things you told them; others they just figured out.

If you have some accomplishments, don't forget your people

If you go off to college, that doesn't make you better than those you left in the neighborhood. For example, if your parents buy you a new car and then you drive right past the people you have met at the bus stop for years, that's not right. That's not keeping it real.

What about those so called "friends" who watch you self-destruct? These are the people who you make take a test that they don't know they're taking. For example, you tell one of your buddies you're going to start selling drugs. He responds with silence. Is that a friend? If I said something like that, I would expect a true friend to knock me out. Watch these types. They're cheerleaders for your failure. That's right. Some people with whom you hang around are planning your nothingness. Isn't that scary? Be careful. Everybody doesn't want you to be successful.

However, all of your associates are not bad. There are some friends out there who may care more about you than some members of your family. Some have done so much for you they should have your last name. They stay up with you late at night. They buy you that meal they cannot afford. You wonder what you would do if you were to lose their relationship. People such as this understand how to stand and cheer for you while the other fellow is the star.

I'm reminded of a person like that in my life. His name is John Crews, Jr. We played high school football and attended college together. We give each other continuous support and serve as constant reminders of each other's struggle. I cannot remember one single argument or a disagreement over a woman. We care and give sincere advice on matters before us. It is this type of relationship that fosters true bonds.

For me, there are some people I know pretty well that I would never borrow five dollars from or trust them in the same room with me if I were blind. Everything a person says or does is not a mistake. Guard yourselves against these negative people. Author, Alice Walker, once said, "No person is your friend who demands your silence, or denies your right to grow." Ask questions and disagree if you have to. Be careful who you hang around. You are charged with the responsibility of choosing your friends wisely.

The last element I want to address in this chapter is telling others our business. Sometimes we talk too much about who we are. Often we tell stories which are uninvited and leave people wondering, "Why do I hang with this person?" A friend already knows your tendencies; so stop talking so much. Our mouths are just too big. People do not have to know all of the things you present to them. Just live your life according to your purpose. It's OK to discuss and exchange ideas but leave all the drama at home.

My father always told me, "If you want to find out about people, just listen to them; they will tell you everything you want to know." Be honest with yourself. People have to earn your friendship and you should earn theirs. *It's all about you.*

Seven

Parents

Remember, your parents gave you the blessing of lips; speak to them with an attitude of gratefulness. —Iyanla Vanzant

Young people, your parents are among the most important people you will ever meet. For me, my parents were the first Black people I met. That alone makes them real special

Parents protect, counsel and give constant feedback that adds to your development. In one of my training sessions, I asked a group of sixth grade boys, "Why do we disrespect the people who provide food, clothing and shelter for us?"

After they stopped and thought about the question, most replied, "It's stupid to be that way."

One young adult even said, "I'm going to stop doing that because they give me everything."

Have you ever gone to your parents and thanked them for being a parent? That would make their day. When is the last time you told your parents that you love them? These activities only take a small amount of time but leave a feeling that parents can't even describe.

For African-American parents, their job encompasses a variety of subjects that have to be addressed. Racism is one of those subjects. How do Black parents teach their youth that people will treat them a certain way based on their skin color? Often parents in this group look at their newborn and think of all of the hardships that he or she will have to encounter. They implement strategies based on their available resources to make sure their children live prosperous lives. The Black mother, based on historical evidence, is shown to have raised many children in America. She was sexually exploited then left to raise her children.

It was very apparent in earlier days that the Black women,

in some instances, had more power over the whole plantation than the European women. It was nothing for a Black woman to breast feed a European baby and a Black baby at the same time. Do you think a European woman would breast feed a Black baby in those days? Of course not.

Young people, there is no way you can get over on your mother. She knows you. Remember, you came from her. She may never let you know that she knows, but she does. In the Black community, there is a constant reminder to all young adults. Don't you always hear from your parents or guardians that they want you to live better than they did? I think that is so unselfish. We have to learn how to appreciate and value our parents.

One sign of excellent parents is when they're doing everything humanly possible to prevent their children from failing. At a middle school here in Greensboro, I am a volunteer football coach. One day during practice, a lady came on the field and said, "Coach, why has Arnold been missing practice; was he cut or something?"

I responded, "No," and looked at Arnold who was standing right beside his mother. Then I said, "Arnold decided himself that he was going to leave the football team."

She looked at her son like my mother looked at me when I swept the kitchen floor debris into the floor vent. She then said, "Coach I'm not letting my son quit this team. His tail will be out here tomorrow. He is going to play."

I was moved when I went home that evening. That is what I call a caring African-American parent. She refused to let her son quit. She made sure he didn't experience failure.

Another sign of an excellent parent is support. You would not believe how many young men on that football team made plays and looked up into the stands. They were looking for their parents. I, along with other coaches, could tell the difference in the kids' performances if their parents were there.

In high school, I played defensive back on the football team. One night I picked off a pass and ran it back for a touchdown. When I entered the end zone, my teammates met me and we started dancing. I was so happy and proud of myself. But guess who was happier than I was? Arriving home later that evening my father met me in the door. He said, "Man, you gotcha one." My father was so happy and proud of me. It is that support that energizes us to continue on our positive paths.

What about those young people whose parents are not there? These are the parents who, if they walked past, their children would not recognize them; parents who don't seem to care and tell their kids they are mistakes; who say to their kids, as Hobson and Hobson assert in their book, *Different and Wonderful*, "I don't like this makeup; it makes me look darker." The authors feel, and I agree, that this experience teaches children that having dark skin is bad.

Certainly, youngsters who live with this kind of orientation, and sometimes even worse, face a challenging life. To tell them we understand is fake. We don't understand if we have not lived under those experiences. The real tragedy is, these young people may blame themselves. They say to themselves, "I don't matter because my parents don't care."

Parents can make children feel helpless or useless. While many kids are obtaining help from a parent who listens to a speech they have written, other kids have written several speeches on hard knocks alone. Many children, right before school starts, look forward to school shopping with their parents. Others take a cab, train, bus or even walk and shop by themselves. Most young adults receive lunch money from their parents. But there are many children who leave their dwelling and go to a neighbor and ask for milk money.

How can a parent, as writer Jonathan Kozol asserts, help a child with homework when the parent can't read? A parent's personal battles can cause continuous hurt and pain to the child. There are many children who do poorly in English class but write wonderful letters to their parents from prison. There are children in school who do poorly in math but help their parents divide crack into grams, etc. This has to stop. Young people, you know right from wrong.

Commit yourself to the thought that you will respect your parents. Try very hard to listen to their advice. Parental experience is so honest. For those of you who find yourselves in terrible situations, it is not your fault. But you will be OK too, because you are learning what not to be, which is equally important. I encourage you to find role models and stay close by them. Local fraternities and sororities, older people in church and even neighborhood friends can help you in your development. You can and will make it. Ask for help. Believe that you can be successful and remember, you deserve better. *It's all about you.*

Eight

Fear

Action cures fear.
        —David Schwartz

*I*n our minds we feed ourselves thoughts of hopelessness.
We question our ability and hide from experiences that will
enhance our lives. Why is this so? Many times it is because we

start fearing the outcomes. We worry about how others may feel which causes us to live according to outsiders. Risk-taking thus becomes a distant memory.

Many young people with great ideas and stories hide behind their fears and cheat everyone else out of their greatness. Their potential dissipates like lonely rain falling from the sky. Young adults, especially in the African-American community, don't apply effective effort because they are scared to fail. Some find themselves lost in the classroom like fish traveling in polluted water. Many are afraid to answer questions in class for fear their peers will think they are smart.

Alas, their environment teaches that they must be "hard." This orientation warns that physical confrontation will happen, so be prepared. In reality, it's just young people who are afraid of each other and who act out in destructive ways because they have not considered other options.

Defeat thus becomes our topic sentence. At a very early age we stop living. We surrender and throw in the white towel all because we fear our expected outcomes. Notice how the white towel signifies giving up which I think is interesting in itself.

As young adults, we are often asked what we want to be in life and we answer very confidently and earnestly. But immediately afterward, we question who we are. All of us have said, 'Oh I can't do that." It is important to note that this has nothing to do with our ability. These feelings make us distrust ourselves. Therefore, we lose before we even take the field because we are fearful.

David Schwartz believes action cures fear. When you're chasing a dream and negative emotions surface; just do it. By the time you remember you are scared, you will have accomplished your task. Think about all the people who commit crimes. They are fearful people, but for periods of time they forget they are fearful and act out in self-defeating behavior. It is the same thing for positive, successful people. They seemingly forget they are fearful and do it. They don't hesitate to return phone calls. They sit in front of the classroom. People like this answer questions in class. They accomplish good things because fear does not grasp them. This is how all of us should learn to live. Controlling this emotion promises opportunities.

Would you believe some people fear being successful? They are not hard to find. Look at all of your associates who have the potential but choose to live different lives. People like this think they can't handle the pressures and so they fail intentionally. That's sad. Human possibility is endless. You can't measure a man's capacity. When he controls himself, he can invent and construct anything he wants.

Since all of us are unique, we fear different things. However, the solution is the same. Folks, action cures it. Moving step by step is the key. A.L. Williams, a prominent entrepreneur, once said, "Inch by inch, it is a cinch." Please do not consider yourself abnormal for these feelings of fear. They are normal. But what separates you from others is your ability to cope and move forward. If I ever fail at something it will be because I didn't apply effective effort; not because I gave up on myself or because I didn't even try.

My parents have a large back yard. There are woods that separate a dirty body of water from their premises. One day I was cutting grass and I saw a snake. Of course, I thought it was from the water. I was so scared because I feared snakes. On this particular day, I ran to my neighbor's house and asked for Mr. Shears. He was there, and we went to kill it. Actually, he was the only one who had a hoe. Mr. Shears found it and destroyed the poor thing. I finished cutting the grass and went inside.

The next week it was time to cut the grass again. I was paranoid, especially at the location where the snake had been spotted. My first inclination was to avoid that part of the yard. Then I remembered what I tell young adults: "Confront your fears head on." So on this day, I decided I would first cut the area of the yard where the snake was spotted. It was difficult but I did it. I even told myself that if I saw a snake this time I was going to kill it by myself. This is what you have to do. Never let fear keep you from doing your job.

We know that we are on track when our fear hides from us. Life is fun when depression sleeps and frustration grows mute. Self-doubt is the child of fear. Remember, when you adopt this way to live, all your goals and dreams are as close as your reach. Fear is nothing more than a test. All of us should pass, for each person makes up his or her own questions. What makes life so great is you keep your own score. *It's all about you.*

Nine

Discrimination

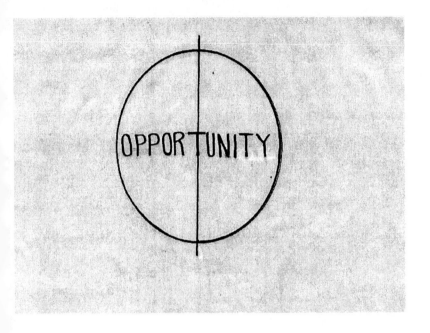

There is no good time to be Black in America, but some times are worse than others. —David Bradley

I n this country, minorities are treated differently than other people. Opportunities, as well as resources, are hidden like a person's suppressed feelings. Life for minorities is filled with struggles as they search for protection. Being Black in this country often suggests "staying in your place." This unwritten law is a constant reminder that Blacks and other ethnic groups are supposed to have limits. With this in mind, maintaining one's motivation can be as distant as the stars. We try not to try, all because we have been told from generation to generation that we are not human. Being oppressed induces a poison that only time can immunize. You know things are terrible when people try to live outside of their own skin color. Black is beautiful.

Passing as White just to shop and buy gasoline was tragic. Classifying people as property clearly shows some people's sickness. If we really were inferior, people would not have set laws that prohibited Blacks from learning how to read and write. Inferior means lower than standard or not having ability. Maybe these law makers knew Blacks had equal ability.

Lewis Terman, in his book, *The Measurement of Intelligence* asks, "Are the inferior races really inferior or are they merely unfortunate in their lack of opportunity to learn?" This belief that one group is intellectually superior is just an illusion. If people are as smart as they say they are, I wish they would compete on equal terms, not by stacking the deck in textbooks, public schools and corporations. For once, people should advance because of their effort and not from keeping other people down.

By now, I guess it's apparent minorities are becoming educated. Black people, in particular, are standing tall and strong. Young brothers and sisters enter and graduate from schools which constantly reflect discrimination. For example, today there are Black graduates from George Washington High School. I wonder if people know George Washington owned slaves? How do adults expect young people to ever appreciate a school when it honors a slave-master? Wasn't he also the first president? Most adults do not believe young adults can see this, but they can. Think about the faces of dead presidents on U.S. currency. Sounds to me like another reminder. Young adults know when something is not designed for them. Remember they talk to each other. They see the visible differences in schools, books and opportunities.

In a training session, I asked a group of young men if they had ever experienced discrimination. One replied, "I walked into a store and they followed me around as if I was going to steal something." He further stated, "The sad thing was I had money." The young man then asked, "Mr. Barksdale, if they treat me like this, what about those who have no money?"

This particular young man was in the sixth grade. What did this experience teach him? It taught him he doesn't matter and that no matter what he does, people will rush to judgment. In his eyes, I could see hate. In the same session, one of his classmates articulated that one time he earned a perfect score on his spelling test. The teacher, in disbelief, walked him outside and said, "Now tell me, whose paper did you cheat off of."

These illustrations are nothing new. Many of the cases described above never get talked about. Many textbooks and teachers are prejudiced against people of color. Low expectations are the root of racism. This is just reality folks. We have to talk and deal with it.

But for the rest of this chapter, I want to approach discrimination differently. I want to talk about what young people do to themselves. How many young Blacks think they discriminate against themselves? Most would think they don't. But, in fact, some of us really do. Young people, every time you choose not to do your homework, you are going against yourself. You may say, "But those lessons are not meant for me. I can go through school for thirteen years and still never uncover who I really am."

Although the above statements may have merit, you do know of the public library. Do you know how to demand that your teachers teach you about your past? Are you open to clearing your mind of feeble thoughts and continue to learn? See, when you try to be cool with the boys, that's discrimination. You are Black and you are already cool. When you don't apply effective effort, you are working against yourself. Can this be changed? Yes it can. How? First, you have to hold yourself accountable for your actions and inactions. Understand that every action has a consequence.

Young brothers and sisters usually say White people deny them opportunities. Believe me, history supports this view. However, before White people get to us, we are often planning our own destruction. We have this thing about carrying protection. Guns. I am here to tell you I carry my own protection everyday. It even has a special name. I call it My Mind. That's right. I use it to read, write and think.

What is this about being bad? Bad is when you can make a computer sing; bad is when you read your mind's book; when you see your imagination; when you touch your potential. Being bad is not killing more people than you have killed ants. Bad is not when you handle more drugs than a pharmacist or steal as an occupation.

I think bad is when you speak and the clouds clap; and when you write, the oceans read and the mountains bow. Bad is when you sing and birds chirp. Again, bad is when you walk and the ground smiles. Bad is when you drive and traffic signs wave. Bad is when your goals breathe. That means they live. How do you define bad?

We have to get out of the mindset that somebody owes us something. What you achieve or fail to achieve is directly related to what you do or fail to do. Your life is what you make it. All you can do is all you can do. But how many of us practice this? Think for a moment. Have you done all you can do? Only you know, so please listen to yourself.

Difficulties, racism and hard times are just as real as what you see. So what? Nothing can hold you back if you just stop standing on yourself. My young brothers and sisters, let's stop running towards nowhere. As Perry Yeoman, a close friend, says, "Tell yourself every morning, 'I am the best thing happening.'"

There are so many opportunities out there. You have the opportunity to be rich or poor, a winner or loser, an asset or liability to society. It's your decision. What you decide will show in due season. *It's all about you.*

Ten

Complexes

No two people on earth are alike, and it's got to be that way in music or it isn't music. —Billie Holiday

When I was in the seventh grade, my father took me to the eye doctor. During the examination I learned I needed glasses. Of course, I didn't like that because I felt the glasses would make me look funny. Days passed and soon I developed a complex. I felt people would call me four-eyes and I didn't want that. That was a tough time for me.

As I grew older I realized everyone has physical characteristics they wish they could change or make disappear. Our friends and neighbors often don't know this because we keep it a secret. When people pick on us, we start asking ourselves self-consciously if we were made right. When this happens, we try to memorize everyone's conclusions except our own. We laugh and joke, but when we find ourselves alone, it hurts our feelings. How do we deal with our complexes? Can we overcome these feelings that hamper our progress?

The first way to deal with your complexes is to admit that you have them. Many times we don't know what we don't know. By uncovering our complexes, we empower ourselves to resolve our own dilemmas. Next, we must uncover the root cause for our hang-ups and change our outlook. Doing this teaches responsibility and self-awareness. The best education is that which is self-taught. Working through complexes teaches us to depend on ourselves for our resolutions.

Young people, remember, all of us deal with the above situations everyday. So you are not alone in this challenge. People are concerned about their weight, hair, skin and clothes. These concerns can cause us to live behind a mask all of our lives. There are a lot of people who celebrate Halloween all year. There's a young lady I know who believes she is unattractive

She puts on layers upon layers of makeup each day. What she's really doing is hiding behind something that gives her false protection.

Young men often find themselves engaging in sports because they have developed a complex about academics. During high school, I had a phobia about math. I believed I was not good in it. Every time I took a test, I would get so nervous and scared. I didn't believe I could do it. If I made a decent grade, I told myself I was lucky. If I flunked the test, I told myself I was dumb or a failure. This was very tough for me because, ever since second grade, I felt teachers were comparing me to Taiwan, my twin sister. So, very early in my development I felt I had to be as smart as Taiwan.

Now I know that during all those years, I was living with a complex—the complex of trying to be like Taiwan instead of myself. It never occurred to me to look at myself for my own talents. I did not value what I did as important regardless of what others said. This is how you get rid of those complexes. Believing in yourself and working hard to develop your skills and abilities will ensure a more successful life. Also, having those inner conversations with ourselves cause us to listen to our own voices.

For those of us in the education arena, I think it's important to understand that young people develop complexes very early in life. This problem effects the learning process. A lot of the problems in young people stem from emotional and social baggage. It's sad, but a lot of young people are labeled dumb, not because they are, but because they are hiding from something and as a result don't concentrate on their work. Adults have to understand this. "Kids play the dozens," parents make comments, and the TV is on all the time. All of these situations provide fertilizer for complexes to grow.

There was a young lady in my fifth grade class who had a severe stuttering problem. The boys and I picked on her everyday. The teacher, Mrs. Poole, would call on her from time to time to read. When she started reading, no one could understand her. Thinking back, she cried worse than a baby whose candy was stolen. Since I have matured I understand that I helped shape her complex. The way we picked on her, she probably will always think she is abnormal. That was not right. We all had problems. That was the same school year when I was afraid to wear the shoes my mother bought me. Another guy who picked on her couldn't read his own name. Another one faced the challenge of controlling weight. So, as you can see, everybody had something they were hiding from. Generally, we pick on others so people won't pick on us.

One of my closest friends had a major complex. He was dealing with the problem of his hair line. As a matter of fact this guy's hair line was so uneven that it looked like he had two foreheads. His stuff was messed up. The fellows around the neigh borhood would pick on him so bad he wouldn't come outside. One of my boys even told him that his hair line and eye brows connected. It took him years to get over this, but imagine how he felt. It is your ability to cope and get over your complexes that shape your self-esteem.

One last point on this subject and we will move on. One bright day, my third grade class ate lunch and then went to run a lap around the school. It was nothing out of the ordinary; we did it everyday. But on this one particular day I told my teacher, "I can't make it around; I have to use the bathroom." She didn't believe me and refused to let me go. I started running and soon after I felt a rush like people going Christmas shopping the day after Thanksgiving. I used the bathroom on myself. That's right, a number two. I went to the bathroom and washed as best I could.

When class resumed the teacher went around checking homework. She looked over my shoulder and checked me off in her grade book. Then she made an announcement, "Children you better check your shoes. I think somebody stepped in dog poo."

I sat there very quietly, but embarrassed. All day I went around smelling like bowel movement. "Why?" The reason was I didn't want anyone to know I used the bathroom on myself. A complex developed so fast I didn't think. All I had to do was call my parents and tell them what had happened. See, when complexes form they distort our realities. We don't think rationally. We put ourselves under unnecessary duress.

Isn't that something? I went the rest of the day like that only because I didn't want others to know I made a mistake. We put ourselves through so much and we lose in the long run. Accept that you have some improvements you want to make and move on.

Your life is far more important than your view of your physical appearance. By taking time to understand yourself, you will develop a shield against potential complexes. You have to do it and you can. *It's all about you.*

Eleven

Regret

I've learned that I don't feel my age as long as I focus on my dreams instead of on my regrets. Live and Learn and Pass It On.

—Unknown

Have you ever regretted something in your life? We often tell ourselves, "If I had to do it all over again, I would change this and that." The tragedy for some of us is that when we hear this, it's too late. Usually, our outcomes were controlled by others. Let me share with you my best friend's comments on some of his regrets. This is the same guy who helped me destroy that club house. In a letter to me, he wrote:

Tommy, What's up?

How are you and your family doing? I hope well. Tell your mom, dad, and sisters that I said, "Hello." Tommy, I haven't forgotten you. You are my best friend and have always been since day one. Tommy, you are a friend of mine for life. If something was to ever happen to you, I would go crazy. Our friendship is very special and important to me. I miss you with your crazy self. I wish we would have hung out together more often; maybe we can when I get out. I'm changing my life around for the best, I'm giving myself to the Lord. Tommy, I will be finished with school next month. After I finish school I'm thinking about starting college. When I get out of prison, I'm going to help kids. I want to talk to them and teach them right from wrong so they won't end up like me, because it isn't worth it. I want to be able to put them on the right path.

Tommy, I don't want anyone to go through what I'm going through now. I had fun in the past hanging out and doing stuff with thugs, but now I have realized that it wasn't worth it. I took the wrong path but now I'm on the right path. Tommy, I hope when I get out that we can help and teach kids together. Helping kids is a good thing. I have three kids (one boy and two girls) of my own. I love them so much and I only want the best for all of them. I'm trying to get out so I can hurry and teach them right before it's too late. Man, I miss you a whole lot and I hope to see you soon.

Very touching isn't it? It didn't have to be that way and he knows that. Young people, if we only do what we are supposed to do the first time, letters such as this would not be written.

Your life is no guarantee. If you believe this, you will also believe that to waste time should be a crime. Many adults say, "If I were younger, I would do this over." Well, they can't. As young people, we should learn from these individuals. See, most of us think we are bigger than time. Keep thinking that way and watch what happens. We must go after our dreams and goals right now. This is a great time to be living.

Les Brown, motivational speaker, told of a story about an older woman that he met during one of his seminars. The topic was about living your dreams and controlling your fear. The lady stood up and said, "If I had to live my life over again I would . . .[etc.]" Clearly she's living with a regret. She let other things get in her way and cheated herself out of life.

One of my closest boys, Damon Johnson, said, "Tommy, I have so much I want to do I should be three or four people." With that attitude Damon will use life up. We all should aspire to live this way. Today is the day that we should act on our dreams and set bigger goals.

George Fraser, in his book, *Success Runs In Our Race,* said, "Delay is not OK." Write that down and adopt it in your life. We have to acquire a larger vision of ourselves that motivates us to want to be somebody. Wasting time is not the answer. Going to prison is taking opportunities away from us. Wil Brower, a Management Consultant, often asks young people in our training sessions, "Why would you give someone complete control over the rest of your life by acting in negative ways?" I have a partner who got in some trouble because his twin brother was killed. Here are some of his comments about his life and regrets in a letter to me.

Tommy, what's up Bro?

I was surprised to hear your voice on the phone. I wish I was out there chillin' with you, Bro. Tommy, man I am trying to maintain in this prison. Hopefully, they will let me go very soon. I am under the old law: twenty years cut to ten years which you only do two and a half. Bro, when I get out I'm starting all over. There are so many places I want to see, and things I want to do. Yes,

I have done wrong in the eyes of some people, but only God can judge me. Everybody else don't count. The Lord knows I have changed. These court judges can't judge me, only God. Take care. Homie for life.

P.S. Send me some pictures.

I issue you a challenge today to live regret free. If and when you do this your life will take on new dimensions. You are in the early morning of your life which means you have all day to make it. You can. Brothers and sisters, if we take time out and apply effective effort, we can make it. Now, be careful, because a lot of people around us look like they're successful. They drive the nice cars and have the stylish clothes. They seem to always play the right music and even have money in their pockets. What does that have to do with you? Learn all you can when you can and develop that mind. Living for today does not insure the future. Remember, it is our responsibility to obtain a larger vision of ourselves despite our odds.

Whatever your background or where you come from, to live with a regret is a burden. Exhaust all your energy in what you want to become and one day you will be able to look back and say, "I did it." *It's all about you.*

Twelve

Crime

Black on Black crime has reached a critical level that threatens our existence as a people. It is a threat to our youths, to our women, to our senior citizens, to our institutions, to our values. And although we are not responsible for the external factors that systematically create breeding grounds for social disorder, we cannot avoid the internal responsibility of doing everything we can to solve the problem that is rending the fabric of our lives. —John Johnson

C rime is a subject that I could write a whole book about. It is my belief that people will behave like they are treated. If they feel like they don't belong, they will act out as such. When we feel like we are less than equal, we carry ourselves like that. Can this be changed? This system is set up whereby only a fraction of us are supposed to be successful. Everybody has the same basic needs: food, shelter and clothing. So, why are so many people hungry, broke and depressed? Why do the "haves" continue to get rich and the "have nots" continue to stay poor if we are all in this together?

The answer lies within each individual. In order to survive, all basic needs have to be met. When we feel we can't get them honestly we commit crimes—all because we want the quick fix instead of working hard and being determined.

It is my opinion, that many criminals never get tried in the court of law. These people commit some of the most hideous crimes ever imagined and nothing happens. You and I pass these people everyday. When we see them, observation alone will not tell us that they're habitual felons. They look, dress and even talk just like us. Who are these people? Can you protect your family and friends from these criminals?

To prepare you to handle these criminals, if you should come into contact with them, I'll give you a few characteristics of these individuals. These people that I'm talking about steal from themselves. They steal from themselves their dignity and integrity. They kill their minds with negative thinking and low expectations of themselves. These criminals commit perjury to their own conscious. They rape other people's opportunities because they are lazy. These people give themselves the death penalty. They give themselves parole by cheating on tests, ignoring teachers and disrespecting parents. Do you know anyone like this? Do you know these individuals have criminal records longer than a twenty mile stretch of highway?

Many people are unaware of their criminal activity. This is because day-to-day it appears that they are successful. To them everything seems to be running smoothly. Life in these times couldn't be better. Thus, goal setting and future planning are not practiced because things are seemingly going so well. These types of people ask, "What's the need?" But as soon as hard times approach, like a quiet storm not fully capable of generating power, they become scared and tense up like a dog visiting a veterinarian.

It's our core values that will protect us from becoming a criminal to ourselves. Our concept of how we want to live gives us tools by which to shape and build our futures. One summer I served as a counselor for a summer program. One young man, a high school senior, told me he wanted to die and he didn't care about living. He was so angry at the world, he wanted to give up. He felt people wouldn't miss him, so why not. He told me he sold drugs but earned an 1150 on the SAT. I learned many young ladies were interested in him. He had more Polo brand clothing than the Polo warehouse stored. So clothes were not the issue. He had many friends-so he said. I met his mother and I could tell she loved him. So what was going wrong? Why was he committing self-destruction?

Young people, he was trying to hang with thugs. In his mind, he felt that was the way to live. Although he had ability and could have channeled his energy other places, he didn't. This is one of the biggest crimes we commit—that is, living outside of who we really are. As you can see, he had potential, but nobody ever knew it. Ask yourself: Am I a criminal? Is my mind captive in my own selfishness? If so, what are you going to do about it? Will you change or stay the same? You have only one life to live and you should live it with a guiding light. You can make it. Say you can. *It's all about you.*

Thirteen

Blindness

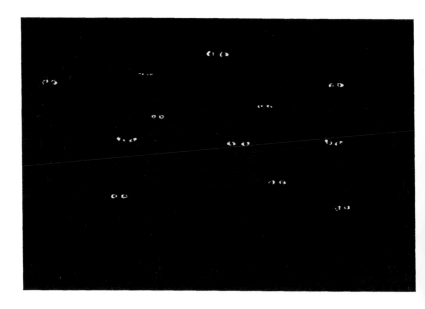

I am invisible, understand simply because people refuse to see me. —Ralph Ellison

W hen we first think of blindness we think of famous entertainers. Ray Charles, Ronnie Milsap and Stevie Wonder come to mind. We often feel a deep compassion for these people, while at the same time wondering what it would be like. As we ponder over this issue, we give thanks for our ability to see and for the use of our other senses. Can you recall a time when you closed your eyes and imagined being blind? While doing this you tried to see. You remember seeing dark, or what you thought was dark, and quickly opened your eyes. Then you breathed a sigh of relief. All of us have done this before.

Living in this short life makes us question its fairness. Seeing those who are disabled induces us to take an inventory of ourselves to see if we are taking life for granted. But just like in the chapter discussing crime, let's focus on us. There are many people that have the ability to see but for many reasons they are "blind." If they were to look at themselves in the mirror, they would see a stranger.

Usually, the people that I'm speaking of have potential but refuse to use it. Some recognize their greatness, others couldn't find themselves if they were alone. They can't see because their minds are like cars in a traffic jam: stuck and helpless. As young people, it seems hard to prosper, but it isn't if we just give ourselves room to grow.

Worrying is one cause of this kind of blindness. Winston Churchill said, "When I look back on my worries, I remember the story of the old man who said on his deathbed that he had a lot of trouble in his life, most of which never happened." We worry so much about that which we cannot control and we lose sight of our purpose. Not having the ability to live by our mission is one sign that we need glasses. By focusing on things that really don't matter, our creative potential is lost like a grain of sand resting at the bottom of the ocean—all because we worry.

Another cause of blindness is the inability to use our heads. We just don't think positive. If we always look down, we should expect to stay down. Many people get wrapped up in poor behaviors just to fit in or be accepted. This commonality distorts our concept of truth and we focus on bad things. Again, we can't see the opportunities before us because we are not looking for growth and development. Coming out of a restaurant one day, I heard one man greet another by saying, "If I had your head I would turn mine in." Although the gentleman was probably just talking, what can we learn from his statement?

One way to insure we stay focused is to never compare ourselves to others. We should always appreciate what we possess and celebrate our happiness. Although the gentleman said he would turn his head in, in reality, he can't. What you are born with is all that you have. Our bodies oftentimes need maintenance, but what you see is what you get. You cannot turn in one part of your body because you don't like the way it looks. That's why a clear concept of self is crucial to a successful life. You have no time to cheat yourself. That's how serious personal development is.

What is another cause of people not being able to see their

talents and potential? One that comes to my mind is working hard at the wrong things. Many of us, young and old, work very hard. However, our work is allocated toward things that give us negative results. We guard ourselves from working at the wrong things by making ourselves our best friend. When we do this, we motivate ourselves and constantly question our efforts. Messages travel within us channeling positive reinforcement back to our values which sustain us.

Also, by believing in our dreams and aspirations, it helps us to move closer to our potential. This is where most of us are tested. Do we truly believe in ourselves? Are we strong enough to prosper over small struggles? Do we have a larger vision of who we are and what we want to become? Young people, note that we are not discussing our eyes and their inability to see. We are focusing on how you view yourself and the different experiences you encounter. We should always trust our mind's eye, which breeds nutrients of motivation. We are tapping into our inner environment, which causes us to feel, think and breathe confidence.

We have the responsibility to guard ourselves against forces that are not in our best interest. We must understand that our development is a serious matter, not to be taken lightly or with a grain of salt. We must acquire an awareness of who we really are. It's very hard to do this when we can't see ourselves. Controlling our thoughts and behavior starts us on our path of achievement. Reading books and turning the television off teaches us the value of self-education. Coping and dealing with family, school and friends give us power to trust the person we see in the mirror. This positive living stuff is hard work. The time we put in will determine how we fair. All of us can do it—step-by-step-by-step. *It's all about you.*

Fourteen

Struggle

When you don't know when you have been spit on, it does not matter too much what else you think you know. —Ruth Shays

P arents, educators, politicians and other public figures, this chapter speaks directly to you. It is going to explain the hurt and despair that American children live with, like an adult with a terminal disease. We are going to learn what we've created. For once, we will look at things from the youngster's perspective and listen to their voices. I challenge you to keep an open mind and accept these truths as you sometimes accept the rhetoric that runs rampant regarding young people's issues.

What are young people facing? Why are they labeled "accidents waiting to happen?" These and many other questions often are asked by adults at expensive conferences, whereby the people in attendance help perpetuate hardships. If this country cares for its children, why are so many children walking around like ghosts scaring everyone? Or why does a person suffering from a severe case of amnesia know himself better than a teenager? Why?

Many young people today live in horrible conditions. Some inner city kids appreciate the room of a condemned house like we appreciate a room at the Embassy Suites Hotel. Many have become so accustomed to living with rats that they place food out on the floor almost like some kids do when they leave a snack for Santa Clause. They go to bed at night with cotton balls in their ears so roaches won't crawl in. Kids all across this country go to school with holes in their clothes because these and other rodents are hungry.

Young people get infected with HIV all because they roll over while asleep and get stuck by their addicted parent's needles that lie in the bed. In these times their only medicine is prayer

82

on which they constantly overdose. Running water is as distant to some kids as drinking water is to a nomad. If you want to visit someone living in Third World conditions, just go the ghettos of New York, Houston, Chicago and other major inner cities. You will find depression as the Pledge of Allegiance. Also, motivation is as distant as I am to the clouds.

It's not the youngster's fault that they are born without a chance. I'm speaking of those who are born addicted to drugs. They didn't have a choice. A growing trend in this country is kids born with assigned numbers. Of course, I'm talking about those whose mothers are in prison. I think being locked up before you even open your eyes is unspeakable. But it happens all the time.

Some children get sick and have to treat themselves. Others are so cold in the winter that they rely on their ash to keep them warm. Is the picture getting painted? If not, I have more. What about eating? Fast food restaurants are popular. But for these young people the only thing they order is survival. They are so hungry their stomach talks and sings. Things are pretty bad when your stomach earns a Grammy. We complain when airplanes fly above our homes and wake us up, but urban children hear war. Young Urban Americans don't experience death in Iraq or Bosnia first. They experience this at their bus stop and then we expect them to learn in school the same day.

If you and I get mad when someone cuts in front of us while

driving, how do you think children feel when we cut school programs and resources? Some schools are so poor, young students' laps are considered their desks. The plumbing is so poor in some schools that students think human feces are decorations. Americans didn't wear gas masks in war first. They wore them in some of the poorest public schools because of the stench. We get angry at work when others question our dignity. I wonder if young people feel we care? One day I was talking to an eighth grader who lived in public housing. I asked him, how did he feel about where he lives? He said, "It makes me grow up very fast and I hate the way it smells. It smells like someone died."

During one of my training sessions at a middle school, a young man told me he discovered a dead body in his backyard. This sixth grader will probably be labeled with an attention disorder, all because he has not received any counseling on this matter. I can understand if he daydreams. What if you discovered a body in your backyard? Would you stay in that house the same night? Probably not. But many kids do it all the time.

What does all of this mean? Adults, this is teaching certain kids that they do not count. We are telling them that others are special and that they are just "whatever." We provide excuse for children not to try. Many more stories and truths could be told, but my goal is not to depress you.

My goal is, however, to remind you of the apparent inequali

ties of this country. Adults have created this situation. Things can change, but we first have to recognize that there are some differences. Then we have to start implementing programs after the "powers that be" have spent some quality time in the places that need the change. It is going to take time because the problems didn't start yesterday. These situations have been around for years.

All of this would be fine if everyone had three or four lives. But we all only live once. That is the real tragedy—that young people live like this and it's their only trip around. The despair and hurt that individuals face is inhumane. Folks, speak out against what has and continues to happen. It is our responsibility to raise America's children—all of America's children.

Adults, the smartest people living are children. But we don't listen to them. They say some of the most profound things. Children speak what you and I imagine. They talk what we dream and feel what we hope. They are just that smart. But in this country, a bridge separates the two. On the bridge you have racism, injustice, inequalities, poor resources, homelessness and poverty. Do you really expect a child to travel through all of that and come out on our side? We wouldn't, so why are our expectations of children different from what we expect of ourselves? As we are learning, we are the ones who are misguided.

Everybody is trying to get a notch up on everyone else. While doing this, we forget to raise our children. Parents, you have to raise your children, not the schools. Your job is to serve, not to neglect. One day I was having a meeting with a principal, and a parent and student walked in. The young man had gotten into some trouble. When the mother started talking to the principal the student said, "Shut up, you talk too damn much as it is." The mother then closed her mouth. I thought, if I had said something like that to my father or mother, you wouldn't be reading this book. What happened to the discipline? It's very difficult to raise and teach someone of whom you are afraid.

A guidance counselor told me that a grandfather was caught molesting his grandson. One family she visited had only spoiled bologna in the refrigerator. What is it? I said it before and I will say it again, people behave like they are treated.

Adults, we better shape up or the future will be a big disaster. I encourage us to look inside ourselves and see what we are doing for those who are less fortunate, and please, not just during holidays. Decide that you will help and encourage children that you will be in your young people's lives. Dr. James Dobson author of several books, stresses to people that, "Eventually, you will become the sons and daughters of your children."

I hope our kids don't decide to raise us like we have chosen to raise them. You deserve better and so do they. *It's all about you.*

Fifteen

Education

One's work may be finished someday, but one's education never.
—Alexandra Dumas

A s you grow and mature, what you are able to tell the world will determine your outcome in life. Your ability o provide information for the betterment of others will give meaning to your efforts. Almost everyday you are going to hear someone tell you to get a good education. Develop your mind and obtain special skills and go for it. Success is yours if you only work for it, and more times than not, people will even tell you that you can do it if you just believe. What do these and countless other statements mean to you?

Have you resolved in your own mind why it's important to learn all you can? If not, let me share with you some experiences that I think you'll find interesting. First, as a young person, if you are not learning or developing your mind with your time, then what are you doing? The likelihood is that you are looking for trouble or have found it. So you find yourselves in trouble and wasting opportunities. But sooner or later something is going to happen in your life and you are going to wish you were educated. For example, there was a young man who lost his father. When the lady who designed the funeral pro gram brought a copy over for his approval he said, "I have to trust that what you said about my father is correct because can't read." That is very real.

Alas, the feeling of knowing that you don't know take years off your life. You spend so much time covering up or hiding from the truth. One day a woman had an interview for a job. When I talked to her she was excited and was proud of herself. She felt things were about to change. Finally, she ex pressed, "I will be able to feed my kids." The interview wa scheduled for 9:00 A.M. The woman missed the interview because she said she thought it meant "nine people after me" were going to get interviewed for the job. She didn't feel like she could compete. Even though that wasn't the issue, she didn't have any confidence. Remember in chapter four when we said to always seek proper understanding? You do this by learning how to read. She was poorly educated and couldn't tell time.

The only sure way to obtain proper understanding is to read and read and read. When you do this, you will introduce yourself to many different worlds. Being educated places you among groups of people where you share ideas and knowledge and create a better tomorrow. Schools, churches, parents and friends all teach you. You have to decide what you are going to do with these and other opportunities.

Like most things in life, education is fine, but you have to be educated in the correct things. Of course, I'm not talking about having the best marketing distribution plan to traffic drugs or hunt people. You and I know right from wrong. Our makeup and environment teaches this. So it's no excuse for negative behavior once you understand this. I once heard a teacher say, "Everybody cannot make A's but everybody can behave." I agree with this only if we are taught to live as such.

As you travel throughout your life, the ability to communicate and articulate your thoughts gives you a definite edge over those who cannot. All it takes is effective effort. Being educated results in confidence, and that's priceless. You feel better about who you are and you make others around you better. Go out and learn all you can so you can do what you want to do. You owe it to your mind, body and spirit.

When you do this, opportunities will lend themselves to you. You will start asking yourself if this is really happening. Get serious about your academics and learn beyond the classroom. Be the first person to use your total capacity.

Every night I encourage you go to bed tired. That means all day you've been productive in the correct things. Pay your body back with proper rest. Develop your peace of mind.

I'm excited that you have decided to live your life according to your purpose and goals. See you at success. *It's all about you.*

Sixteen

Why?

For some perverse reason, we children hated those marigolds . . . perhaps we had some dim notion of what we were, and how little chance we had of being anything else. Otherwise, why would we have been so preoccupied with destruction? —Eugenia Collier

Young adults, the word "why" is often the beginning of a question which usually carries a connotation that something negative has happened. We often hear from our parents: why do we do this or that? Our teachers ask us: why did we get in trouble or fail to do our homework? Society asks us: why are we the way that we are? This one word rings in our ears more than holiday bells. In this chapter, we will explore different reasons why we think, feel and act out certain things. By asking several questions, it is my hope that you will honestly probe your mind to explain your version of truth.

The first question that I pose to you is: Why do you exist? Think long and hard before you answer. This is a question that has been asked before. But I want you to tap into yourself and ponder over this question.

Many young adults have told me they exist by mistake. Others feel that they were born for a specific purpose. Some say they exist because everyone else does. And the one reason that I find most interesting, is, a few feel they exist because someone has to be bad or cause the trouble.

This last reason is where I want to spend some time, because living with this orientation is dangerous. It's a cold reality that young adults feel this way. Those who live like this believe that what they do is rational. They believe that their negative acts and feelings are OK.

I was working with a high school and I asked a group of males what they thought of selling drugs. One guy said, "Man, it's OK as long as I don't hurt anybody."

Another mentioned, "I just do it to make my loot; I have to get mine."

If you are in disbelief by these attitudes, let me say that they are as real as a depressed person believing if they die the world will be a better place.

Nobody is born to cause trouble or harm. When we find people feeling like this, especially young people, they are hiding from something or covering up to protect a complex. Some are hurting from the death of a loved one, breakup, low grades in school or divorced parents. They become frustrated because they believe no matter what they do nothing good will happen. When this happens, people become helpless. In their minds they feel they do not control their outcomes. Students like this don't try to improve because they have learned to become passive. They sing songs of defeat and play chords of hopelessness.

We can protect ourselves from these feelings by developing our own concept of who we are. Taking time to discover our internal controls, breeds happiness, confidence and hope. Write down your thoughts and ask yourself questions. Then and only then will you start obtaining an awareness of self.

When Wil Brower and I train young people in a program called STEP-UPP (Success Through Effective Participation Utilizing Positive Potential), we often hear young black males talk of becoming professional athletes. Why is this so? While coaching I discovered I could encourage a young person to lay everything on the line in football but he will not do that in the classroom for his teacher. These young people would easily get excited about practice but when I asked them about their grades, they looked at me as though I was talking bad about their mother. They can perform in the classroom but what they tell themselves about their academics is where they lose.

Understand that if a person fails in school, that does not make him a failure as an individual. But what happens is that young adults experience one failure and they give up. Those young guys who played football, who, I might add, won the city championship that year, didn't do too well academically. Why? Effective effort was not practiced in the classroom as on the field and they couldn't find a reward for doing well. Young people, your reward for becoming educated is payment for life's riches. I contend that young Black males can do just as well in the classroom as on the field if they apply themselves.

One of my greatest joys happened after a game when a parent approached me. She said, "Coach, did you know my son had a severe reading problem?"

I replied, "No I'm glad you told me. Is there something that I can do?"

She said, "I appreciate that because, you know, he uses football to help him cope with his problem."

I was so amazed by that. I mention that it was a joy because it taught me that a coach is more than a coach. What I did is what a lot of coaches do but nobody ever talks about it. The next day at practice I talked to him and gave him the STEP-UPP pledge that Wil Brower had designed for the student program. It is a poem that talks directly to young people about living. I explained to him that for twenty minutes, before practice each day, we would read this pledge. I told him that he didn't have a reading problem, and I expected him to practice reading everyday.

One last thing about this story that deserves mentioning is: this young fellow didn't really have a severe reading problem. But everybody kept telling him he had one. Although I don't teach reading, this fellow simply needed assistance—but we all do. We practiced and practiced everyday, and this guy started to feel good about himself. He told himself he had the ability to read and he achieved it!

Why is it that some young people think that getting into trouble is cool? When they see a friend or associate get in trouble, they laugh. For you who like to get into trouble, you're cheating yourself. You cannot imagine the different ways life will take you. Telling me, "I don't care," or "So what?" is unacceptable. You do care, but you are trying to keep it real.

What is "real" anyway? What does "that's the bomb" mean? To me, these are positive slang terms, not negative ones. You do not keep it real when you are walking around higher than a kite. You are not "the bomb" when you can't make a subject and verb agree. It's not "cool" when the warrant officer delivers more mail to you than a mailman. It is not "all good" when you go to school without books. Things are not "butter" when you're always looking over your shoulder because you owe someone money.

Young adults, you know what's up. But it's your choice. *It's all about you.*

Seventeen

Needs

When you plant lettuce, if it does not grow well, you don't blame the lettuce. You look for reasons it is not doing so well. It may need fertilizer or more water or less sun. You never blame the lettuce.

—*Thich Nhat*

E veryday people wake up to their "To Do" lists to accomplish their daily tasks. Whether professionally or personally, these activities are ranked by priority. We tell our friends and colleagues how busy we are and make comments such as, "Time just goes too fast." During the week, we are so consumed by these lists that we can forget what day it is. Then we often wonder what happened to the week. Then we find this week turns into months and then years. And so we start looking back on life, wondering where did it all go.

Relationships, marriages, peers and children cause us to hold in our feelings. While all of these influences seem, at the beginning, to breed happiness for us, we learn we've been putting a band-aid on a wound so deep the surgeon himself has to dive in to operate. This permanent scar is the result of people not taking time out to see what they individually need. Folks, you have to take care of yourself. Talk to yourself. What do you need? That is the question. In order to accomplish what you will, certain tools must be purchased. Well, what are they? If you don't know, nobody else is going to tell you.

Most people go directly through life living for everyone else except themselves. They do everything for everyone else, but nothing for themselves. I learned I was like this at age twelve when I had my lawn mower business. Traveling the neighborhood, I felt that I did quality work. Many customers offered repeat business. Some Saturdays I neglected my own yard to make money, but my father soon corrected my behavior. One day he told me, "Tommy, you should never go and cut someon else's yard when yours looks a mess. What message are you sending?"

This is exactly what I am speaking of. We make everyone else feel better, beautiful and free but our "yards" look so bad we can't see our houses. Think about all the times we cleaned up our dwellings when we learned we were going to have company. After your company left it returned back to a pig sty. Our house should be clean anyway, because we live there. Similarly, we wash our cars when we take a young lady out. But we should wash our car because we are taking ourselves out.

The ability to understand your needs will protect you from foolishness that will creep up on you like the flu. You won't have to question your decision on whom to date, what clothes to buy, when to get married, or even when to get a divorce. It's already worked out. You know what you can handle and what you can't. So make the decision and continue to move forward. When you make these life changing decisions, take Satchel Page's advice. "Don't look back, something may be gaining on you." Move on.

How can we better understand our needs? First, we must believe that we are worthy of great things. Some people don't believe they are deserving of happiness or of riches. If you find yourself feeling like this, go to the mirror and take a deep breath. Look at the top of your head and the bottom of your feet. Then think about how big your bathroom, house, city, state, country and world are. Then ponder over this: what you are looking at is all that you have. As big as things are, realize how small you are compared to other things. But it is not what you have; it's who you are. Physically, you are small, but if your heart and mind are full, that's all you need. You have no time to think you are not worthy. Life will keep going and pass you by.

Next, we must ask ourselves a series of questions. For example, what do you tell yourself about your successes and failures? Do you rely on luck or do you believe in your ability and effort? It's crucial that you understand your makeup. What is your theory of self? We all have to learn our own cures in life.

I challenge you to stop living other people's lives, especially those on TV and in the public eye. We worry about how they are doing and ignore ourselves. You are special because of your uniqueness. If you ever meet a celebrity, you will probably get real excited and tell all your friends. Well, that's fine, but I feel the celebrity should get excited about you too. Do you?

Alas, we have to learn not to make other people's problems ours. This is a very common mistake. We get that one phone call from a person who dumps all of his or her hang-ups and complexes on us. Time after time, they tell us how bad life is and how much money they don't have.

One day, a lady told me her boss hated her, her husband, children and anybody and everybody else hated her. After a couple of minutes passed, I even started to hate her. She was just so negative and pessimistic. Nobody needs that. We may find ourselves not knowing our next step in life, but as long as you know what you don't need, things will work out.

For example, take a person who doesn't like his or her job. They need to quit, but won't because they have gotten married to their Visas, as Jawanza Kunjufu, the author, says. One thing this person should understand is that being depressed is not going to make the situation better. Complaining and blaming the world won't help. Buying a house or a new car is not what they need. That will only make them happy today. I sometimes call that window dressing. Again, I ask: What do you need?

How we decide to handle and acquire our needs is up to us. One thing is for sure, understanding our needs saves us from possible danger. Remember from a previous chapter, we discussed not wanting to live with a failure oriented system? We basically want to enjoy life and be happy. David Thoreau said, "Oh God, to reach the point of death only to realize that I have not lived." That is so serious.

Develop your needs and establish action items for your life's program. None of us have to live in a sea of uncertainty. Make decisions based on your needs. When we learn to do this, our wants will come. Remember, when we play small, we don't serve the world. *It's all about you.*

Eighteen

Choices

If a man can write a better book or preach a better sermon, or
make a better mouse trap than his neighbor, even if he builds his house
in the woods, the world will make a beaten path to its door.

—Ralph Waldo Emerson

 e live by our choices. Some decide to live a life of

quality, while others choose to live with the sign, Insufficient Funds, marked on their minds. This starts very early in development and carries all the way until we reach a point where we're the living dead. Think about all of those who are addicted to drugs, sex and their own concept of life. They made a series of bad choices which caught up with them and twisted their life, spirit and reality. When your mind reads Insufficient Funds, it means nothing is there. It doesn't matter how many times you go to make a withdrawal because you are trying to get something out of nothing. Therefore, you get no personal reward for your efforts. This has to be very disheartening.

Many people with this insufficient orientation blame others for their failure. They often cry that racism is a culprit for why they have not achieved. While this is going on, the situation is not getting any better. Time keeps moving and so does these people's despair. People sometimes mention that where they live makes them choose to do negative things. Is that true? Or are people raised with unfortunate conditions and choose to use that as an excuse to become nothing? One of my college associates told me that he came from the ghetto. He explained that he always had a clear concept of life and self because his mother always told him: "We live in the ghetto, but the ghetto doesn't live in us." This type of thinking is where we are going to spend some time.

Many stories could be told on the following pages about

people who came from meager living and became success stories. Joe Dudley, founder of Dudley Products, Inc., a dear friend, comes to mind. But what I think deserves more attention is the series of choices we make that invite success into our lives. People don't just wake up and become successful. It takes hard work, persistence and a series of the right choices.

How do you know when you are making the correct choices? One of the easiest ways is to see if your activities are in-line with your goals. If you don't have any goals, it's important that you obtain them. Write them down and learn them. Goals provide you with reminders of what and how you should be living. Next, be honest and ask yourself: Do I like who I am and what I'm doing? If you answer no, then it's time to change.

I also encourage you to ask yourself this question, a question that my sixth grade reading teacher, Mrs. Wilson asked: "What will I be doing five years from now if I continue to do what I am doing today?" If you get nervous about your answer, there is a possibility you have made some wrong choices. None of us are perfect so we are going to make mistakes. But here we are speaking of a series of choices that cause our potential to rest. The right choices are critical for you to monitor your development.

Many times over, people will not take personal responsibility for their choices. They let others control their thoughts and beliefs. Young adults, you know you're making correct choices when you start applauding yourself and when you create man positive options for yourself that expand the world over.

One day I was talking to a very close friend of mine named Ray Cooke. We were discussing future plans and ways in which we could grow. I remember telling him that I was proud of his accomplishments and he returned the compliment. I then asked him, "Ray, what made you successful?"

His response was so profound I will never forget it. He said, "Tommy, I made a choice like everyone should, to stop running from my life." Isn't that great? Have you been running from your life? Are you mad because you are you? If you do not know the answers to these questions think about your latest choices. If your activities are not producing positive results, then your choices could be better.

What causes people to make bad choices? Many times we are influenced by our peers and associates. We also find ourselves making emotional decisions without the proper understanding. We guard ourselves from this by obtaining leadership skills for our own lives. To lead yourself, you must define your wants, needs and standards. When you do this, negative things will run from you. This happens because your orientation is positive. You become happier and live a more healthful life.

Another cause of making bad choices is, we don't ask ourselves enough questions. I stress this because your life is yours. Have you every asked yourself, "Are my thoughts and activities n-line with growth and my vision?" It's important that we learn to respond instead of react. Instead of living with apathy—Think!

When you can see that your choices are influencing your goals and aspirations, you are growing. Life will become your big play ground. Consider those times when you made decisions not to do something. You foresaw the negative outcome and stayed away. Times like these are when you really start enjoying who you are. Take time out to monitor your choices in life. Arm yourself with the right tools: choices. If we do not, this is one of the first forms of self-hate. *It's all about you.*

Nineteen

How?

Our nettlesome task is to discover how to organize our strength into compelling power. —Dr. Martin Luther King, Jr.

How can I apply the concepts of the first eighteen chapters to my life? How can I apply any concept to my life? How do I pick myself up and dust myself off? If I lack confidence or just can't seem to be motivated, what should I do? How do you become happy when everything around you is terrible? These are questions that have traveled through all of our minds.

Let's start to answer these questions by stating it's OK not to be where you want to be right now. It's OK to go through struggles. As Ronald Harris, a former teammate and high school friend, once said, "It's OK not to have all your pieces to the puzzle." I have always admired a person who accepts his circumstances as he finds them. Often we must sit down with our problems to see where they come from.

People will try to make you think that you are inadequate because you are going through something. You're not crazy or a failure. Times are just hard. That's life. Some will invite you to their success story parties and tell you all of this stuff. You don't care about all of that and you shouldn't. When you find yourself with a bad attitude tell your mind's ear that this can't last forever. Problems are just problems. We internalize so much that it should be part of our digestive system.

Remove that burden in your own time and space. You are just fine. Think about how you eat cookies or chips. Before you start, you tell yourself I'm only going to eat one or two. Then minutes later, you find yourself eating the whole row or bag. That is the same thing that happens to our struggles and problems. We intake so much of that "stuff" and swallow it and keep it for life. Let it go! It's OK.

Life is fun if we choose to make it that way. One day I wanted to take a female friend out on a date. I was very excited about this and I thought she liked me. As we were making plans it dawned on me that I didn't have any money. So I did something that I don't think most people do. I told her, "Look, we can't go out because I'm broke." I then said, "We probably won't be able to go out for awhile because I don't see any money coming in." I didn't hide behind something, nor did I try to borrow the money. I felt she had to like what I had or didn't have. I mentioned life is fun because you have the right to tell people your status if you choose to. I was so proud that I told her what my situation was. She could have accepted it or left it. She left it.

We control our thoughts and beliefs. When you find your-self with no motivation, figure out what's holding you back. The ability to question ourselves often brings some of the best cures. Don't you get tired when old friends ask you how you are doing or what you are up to? I asked that because I wonder how many honestly care. See, never compare your successes and failures to anyone else's. We are all different.

What about confidence? Do you believe that because of your skin color you don't deserve nice things? Do you feel that because you are on reduced lunch you are made of less quality? Just because you were raised by a single parent, that does not make you any less a person.

Gradually, we should accept these situations in life and learn from these experiences. Your worth is decided by you and no one else. Having confidence in your life experiences teaches you to be optimistic. If you have a set-back, but have confidence, you know that it is only temporary. People with confidence don't take rejection personally, they just persevere.

One thing that all of us forget is to be happy. So many things go on in life that make us docile and feel low. We are so busy with our jobs, school, monetary worries and relationships that we forget to be happy. Many times people possess some of the finer things in life but are not happy. They look good on the outside but internally they cry help. We must enjoy life, because it doesn't last forever.

Can anyone make you happy? Can you find enjoyment from other people? People can help you but folks, being happy is all up to you. Individuals can make you laugh and smile but long-term happiness is your business. See, when you are happy you feel good about yourself and can't believe so many people are down in the dumps. When you involve yourself in happy-oriented activities, you foster relationships with people that last for a life time.

What makes me happy is if I can make those around me happy. A lot of us find ourselves having to be around other people. But again, that is only temporary. If you can't be happy by yourself then you have not learned to appreciate yourself fo enjoyment. I had to learn this. I used to stare at the phone hoping someone would call me. I would even take the phone, in the bathroom with me because I didn't want to miss a call. Several times I would take a shower with the bathroom door open so I could hear the telephone. Isn't that something?

When you are able to accept experiences just as they are and still feel good, you are on that path towards personal mastery. By understanding that, in all things, happiness is crucial, you will gain unlimited power over your struggles. How do you get over those hurdles? It's all in your hands to decide. Stop wearing shades on your heart and mind. The answers are as close to you as your own skin. Tell me "how" you are going to do it. I am waiting to see. *It's all about you.*

Twenty

Conclusion

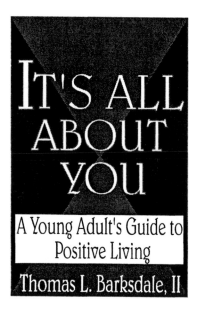

The impulse to dream had been slowly beaten out of me by experience. Now it surged up again and I hungered for books, new ways of looking and seeing. —Richard Wright

I t is my hope that these lessons, concepts and real-life experiences about my life and people with whom I have come into contact, will shed some light on various issues young adults face. We have discussed many situations that all of us can relate to at some stage in our development. If we decide to internalize these learning tools we can prosper to any height of our choice.

To grow, however, we have to value ourselves. Accepting who, what and how we are, encourages a better tomorrow. Until we truly accept this person in the mirror, we invite self-defeating behavior that leads us to misrepresenting our life.

Young adults, if your mind is in the gutter you run the risk of living in one. Control what you think about. Peer pressure and whom you date have nothing to do with your thoughts if you control them. You can do it. One of your full time jobs is to protect yourself from negative people.

Life is difficult. Have you accepted this fact? Whatever your race, everybody has hardships. When we find ourselves wanting to drop out of life, we must hold on. All things work for the good. Remember, change is good, so don't be scared. We can't expect different results if we do the same things. Life is yours to use. Get up off your seat of defeat. Smile at life and say, "Here I come."

As you travel through life, your ability to understand different subjects increases your opportunities. One of the first lessons we should learn is, without proper understanding we are placed in a state filled with limits. Practice patience and gain tolerance of people. Read all you can and take time to explore different worlds. Say you can!

All of us can be winners. There is not a single sole who has to be a loser. We should adopt in our hearts that a winner is one who values all things and learns to appreciate people. Many setbacks are going to happen. A winner fails many times. But if you live by knowing you can make it, you will create your own rewards.

Being competitive is also very important. It's hard, but don't surround yourself with failure-oriented people. They are easy to see; they don't aspire to become anything. They live for the moment and feel life owes them something. Obtain your measures for winning and do it.

I cannot stress enough the importance of hanging with people who are doing something. You are what your friends are. It may look like you are happy with the friendship, but if the two of you are not growing, then you are growing smaller. Some people are cheerleaders for your failure. We don't need to tell everyone our business if we are comfortable with what we are doing. For those who are special to you, protect them in all ways possible

Your parents are some very important people. Love them and appreciate their lives. They give you constant support and feedback. They are such special people. Some of you find yourselves in terrible positions. Tell yourself that you deserve better. Look for role models in your communities and stay very close to them. People care.

114

Conclusion

One of the biggest ways to overcome fear is to act. We all can succeed when we learn to control this emotion. Focusing on our dreams and goals and moving toward them saves us from regrets in the future. Many people fail in life because they are fearful. Their potential is lost within themselves and thus they have negative outcomes. A prosperous and successful life should not be feared. Hard work and dedication help us fight the battle of fear.

Many people fail to recognize that people are just people. Some think that others are inferior which is outrageous. Discrimination is a reality and so we must deal with it. We do this by proving people wrong, not right. One of the biggest crimes that we commit is when we cheat ourselves out of our opportunities. You and I deserve better, so let's act like it.

Every human being has a complex over something. It's normal. If you decide to let it overtake your thinking, you will create problems. Accept that you have some improvements that you want to make and move on. Don't let these feelings control your thinking. You are just fine. Worrying will not help—only self-love.

Living a regret-free life is very meaningful. We protect ourselves from regrets by doing everything possible right now. Decide to commit yourself to developing and acting on your dreams. Many people wake up at some point in their life wishing they could go back and do it over. The reality is they can't. We have to act now and guard against trouble. Ask yourself: What can I do to develop who I am? Write down your mission and your purpose. Prison and getting in trouble are not the answers. Many letters are written everyday by people who tried to be hard and now are locked up. That's not good.

Criminals that we discussed in this work are those who robbed themselves of their dignity and respect. They are captives in their own ignorance and can't find themselves. We should never try to live outside of who we are. Set high expectations for yourself and do what you will.

Are you blind? If you were alone, would you be able to find yourself? Everybody has potential but not many choose to use it. We have to learn that it's our responsibility to maximize our greatness. Outside forces are going to confront you and it's your task to remove these obstacles from your life. You can do it.

Young adults all over this country are living with horrible conditions. They struggle and live a very difficult life. As adults, we should understand this and create opportunities that help young people not to destroy themselves. Parents, teachers and administrators, it is up to you to change these situations. These apparent inequalities continue because people fail to believe that they exist. Until we deal with this head-on, life for many young adults will remain bleak.

Learning all you can will place you further in life. Riches will await you and success will greet you. Your school work is critical step toward your development. Reading outside of the classroom teaches self-education. We all can benefit when one is educated. Have you decided in your own mind why you need to learn? It's your choice. Please answer. Learning is fun because knowledge is power, if you use it. We have to learn to motivate ourselves. We do this by learning as often as we can. Read.

Why do we do certain things? Why even ask why? Think long and hard about this one word. Many people ask themselves "why" after it's too late. I believe that you have now obtained the understanding that you need to prosper. Young adults, your creation is up to you. Why not let it all hang out? Why not be great and obtain riches? Why not build options for yourself that will last a lifetime?

Have you figured out what you need? If you haven't, it's OK, as long as you are aware that this must be addressed. All of us need different things, so don't compare yours to anyone else's. When you write down your needs and work hard to obtain them, you will appreciate your efforts. Those who do for themselves have a deep control over their lives. You and I can work toward this inch by inch.

Choices are made everyday. It will be your ability to make them correctly that fertilizes success. Remember, you define your own success, no one else. Knowing what you stand for gives you power over peer pressure. Please note, you can have peer pressure all by yourself. So many of us choose to take a nap for life.

Our minds are so twisted we hear colors and see sounds. It's not designed to function like that. What choices will you make? You control your outcome.

How does this affect you? By now I hope that you have been charged with the task of accepting the opportunity to have an opportunity. If you refer to these pages as you travel your life's journey, examples and concepts are here to help in time of need.

By reading this work, it already proves that you care about who you are. I am so proud that you stayed the course. Wash your hands of limits, depression, frustration and despair. Brush your teeth of negative attitudes thicker than ten years of plaque. Comb your heart to unwrinkle the love. Wave good-bye to people that cripple your existence. People who paralyze your understanding don't deserve your time. Say to yourself, "Hello my name is, _____. Glad to finally meet you."

See you at Success. I can tell you love you. Let's meet one day. *It's all about you.* Congratulations! One last question: Who would you become if no one else was looking?

Bibliography
&
Suggested Readings

Akbar, Na'im. *Visions For Black Men*. Nashville: Winston-Derek Publishers, Inc., 1991.

Bennett, Lerone, Jr. *Before The Mayflower*. New York: Johnson Publishing Co., 1961.

Brown, Les. *Live Your Dreams*. New York: Avon Books, 1992.

Carson, Ben, M.D., with Cecil Murphey. *Gifted Hands- The Ben Carson Story*. Michigan: Zondervan Publishing House, 1990.

Davis, James. *Who is Black? One Nation's Definition*. Pennsylvania: The Pennsylvania State University, 1991.

Fraser, George. *Success Runs In Our Race - The Complete Guide to Effective Networking in the African American Community*. New York: William Morrow and Company, 1994.

Hobson, Darlene, Derek. *Different and Wonderful: Raising Black Children In A Race Conscious Society.* New York: Prentice Hall Press, 1990.

Jones, Laurie. *Jesus & CEO.* New York: Hyperion, 1995.

Kozol, Johnothan. *Illiterate America.* New York: Anchor Press, 1985.

Kozol, Johnothan. *Amazing Grace: The Lives of Children and the Conscious of a Nation.* New York: Crown, 1995.

Kunjufu, Jawanza. *Countering The Conspiracy to Destroy Black Boys, Volumes 1&2,3.* Chicago: African American Images, 1985.

Peck, Scott, M.D. *The Road Less Traveled.* New York: Simon and Schuster, 1978.

Schwartz, David. *The Magic Of Thinking Big.* California: Wilshire Book Company, 1987.

Seligman, Martin, Ph.D. *Learned Optimism.* New York: Alfred Knopf, 1991.

Smith, Lillian. *Killers Of The Dream.* New York: W.W. Norton & Company, 1949.

Terman, Lewis. *The Measurement of Intelligence.* Boston: Houghton Mifflin Company, 1916.

Bibliography & Suggested Readings

Williams, A.L. *All You Can Do Is All You Can Do, But All You Can Do Is Enough.* Nashville: Oliver Nelson, 1988.

Wilson, Amos. *The Developmental Psychology of the Black Child.* New York: Africana Research Publications, 1978.

About the Author

T homas L. Barksdale, II, is the President and founder of The Barksdale Foundation, a motivational speaking and educational consulting firm. Thomas has reached many young people by working with public schools, churches, outreach programs, civic organizations, universities and associations, instilling values into as many young adult's lives as possible.

From elementary school graduates to managers and CEOs of major corporations, Thomas emphasizes the importance of the human touch. As an advocate of mental stimulation resulting in self-fulfillment, he has developed the key principles of mastery and proactive living.

Thomas is a graduate of North Carolina Agricultural and Technical State University, earning a Bachelor of Science degree in Transportation Management. He lives in Greensboro, North Carolina.